Fasten Your Sweet Belt:

10 Things You Need To Know About

Older Child Adoption

Jodi Jackson Tucker

With

Agnes Tucker

Outskirts Press, Inc.
Denver, Colorado

Fasten Your Sweet Belt
10 Things You Need to Know About Older Child Adoption
All Rights Reserved.
Copyright © 2011 Jodi Jackson Tucker
V3.0

Outskirts Press, Inc.
http://www.outskirtspress.com
ISBN: 978-1-4327-7647-3

Cover Photo by: Karen Lane Photography

Cover Design by: Olivia Jackson

Edited by: Amy Tucker Pyecha

Outskirts Press and the "OP" logo are trademarks belonging to Outskirts Press, Inc.

PRINTED IN THE UNITED STATES OF AMERICA

Dedication

This book is dedicated to adoptive mothers everywhere.

I am standing with you through it all.

I give all glory to God, who first adopted me,

and showed me the power and meaning of

eternal love.

Table of Contents

Introduction

My husband likes to joke that he learned about his three latest children through a text message. I wish I could say that he is kidding, but that is really how it happened.

I was sitting at a conference a few years back listening to the closing session. The first speaker was an inspiring sixteen-year-old adoptee who told his story of being adopted when he was fourteen, after he had given up all hope of finding a family. The next speaker was a prominent missionary who described how she and her husband had adopted three older siblings and what a blessing the kids had been to their family.

And then it just hit me – I knew that my husband and I were meant to adopt an older child. Sitting there alone in the darkened lecture hall, I sent Jerry, my sweet husband, a text that said: *I think there are more children in your future.* His answer: *Call me!* At his age of 53, these were the last words he expected from me. But God had other plans.

Speaking of God, you will see He features prominently in this story. I am a Christian, and I believe adoption is a sacrament ordained by God, so it would be impossible for me to write this book without including Him. I am just here to tell my story the way it happened for me. If you have any faith tradition, you probably believe that your adopted children are a gift from God – how could you not? So, thanks for letting me tell this story from my perspective.

An important disclaimer here: There are many wonderful books about adoption, written by highly qualified experts. I have read most of these, and I recommend that you do the same. These books have been invaluable to, and I could not have weathered the seas of adoption without them. I included a list of some of these in the final pages of this book.

I, on the other hand, am not an expert of any kind. In fact, in reading those books I mostly learned all the things I have done wrong already! So please be sure to read those books -- they are very important.

But adoption is also a funny and crazy and life-changing experience that is a great story no matter how many times I hear it. Each family's story is different and wacky and wonderful. Being an adoptive parent can seem like a daunting, overwhelming task in which you are held up as a model for the rest of the world. But the purpose of this story is to show that even a tragically flawed gal like me can muddle through and have some of the greatest experiences with her kids that life has to offer.

So I hope you enjoy these pages, and that they inspire you to write down your own stories. We can all learn so much from each other.

Blessings,

Jodi

But Ruth replied,
"Don't urge me to leave you
or to turn back from you.
Where you go I will go,
and where you stay I will stay.
Your people will be my people
and your God will be my God."

Ruth 1:16

Lesson 1

Keep It Small – Skip the Mall

(adjusting)

Two days after our kids got home from Uganda, our good friend and neighbor offered to take the girls to the store to buy much-needed hair products for their hair type. (In case you hadn't noticed from the pictures, my girls' hair is not quite the same as mine. There is a whole book that could be written about "hair issues in adoption", but that is another story. One of you can write that one.)

Anyway, this wonderful friend was so gracious in her offer. The girls were just relaxing at home, and it was clear they were still jet lagged and adjusting. So I cautioned my neighbor:

"That sounds wonderful, but the girls are tired, so maybe just that *one store*, OK?"

But my cautioning words were lost in the moment as the girls buzzed excitedly around our friend, dreaming of a trip to a store with this kind lady.

Three hours later, I was standing at the front door waiting for them to come home. Eventually, they arrived and came into the house literally like the walking dead. They were mute, dragging their bags of hair lotion, stumbling into the house. My friend told me that while they were out, she decided to "walk them around the mall" near our home to help them "see where they live."

Honestly, this well-intentioned outing turned out to be a major disaster. I should have declined. I did not know that our kind neighbor's attempts to "orient" them to our community came much too soon, and the girls were not ready. They were zombies, not for the next few hours, but for the next few *days.*

Coming from a developing nation, they simply could not understand or process all they had seen and heard at the enormous mall. Their brains had no way to integrate all the

2

overwhelming stimulation of the shopping complex with all of its stores and electronics and people and endless unfamiliar American images. They had never seen that many cars in their life, much

less all the things inside the stores. They were on complete sensory overload and miserable. They shuffled off to their room and barely spoke for hours.

In fact, not only was a mall too overwhelming for a child from an institutional environment or a simple village, but even our *home* was overwhelming for our kids initially. If you think about it, a young child growing up in America has years to learn the many objects in our living environment and he has time to master them at his own pace with trial and error. But kids arriving here by plane for the first time from a totally different setting have no time to integrate or interact with everyday things we consider common.

Here are just a few of the things that my kids had not experienced and did not understand:

- o   Stairs (as in how to properly traverse them)
- o   Can opener

- o Doorknobs (who knew there were five different ways to open a door just in our one house?)

- o Refrigerator

- o Ice maker

- o Zip lock bags

- o Shower curtain

- o Light switches (our little boy likes to run through the house and turn them ALL ON).

- o Flushable toilet

- o Bras (there could be a whole chapter here!)

This is just a partial list – I could go on and on.

I have to confess...I had been warned about this before my kids came home, but *I just didn't get it.* Many adoption experts tell you to be careful not to "overwhelm" your children with American culture at first, but I just didn't comprehend what this really meant, or how important it was. I thought it meant that I was not to overly schedule them with activities or take them to too many IMAX movies. I didn't really understand just *how much* processing their brains were going to have to do on a daily basis just to adjust. I didn't realize just how *small* I needed to make their world at first to let them slowly learn and cope and master our environment. Like keeping an infant home after birth, older adopted kids need the same transition time to get acclimated.

After watching my kids of varying ages make this transition, here is the analogy I now draw for my children's experience in being adopted:

Imagine you are abducted by aliens and taken to a planet far away. This planet has different terrain, different weather, and even smells differently from Earth – a strange, unfamiliar smell. The aliens speak a strange tongue that you cannot understand. They are constantly looking at you and chattering in their language. You struggle to read their expressions and understand, but you feel mostly confused. The aliens also look different from you, and they are dressed in garments you have never seen. The space ship in which they live is full of objects that you cannot understand. The aliens begin to eat, but you don't recognize any of the foods offered. Although you are hungry, you are too scared to eat. Eventually, you are taken to a room where you are supposed to rest. The bed feels strangely soft and smells funny. You have never laid on anything like this before. Finally, you rest, only to wake up in the morning disoriented and confused, having to face it all again.

Now imagine how exhausted and overwhelmed you--a fully functioning adult--would be after just one day on this "planet." But this is how our older adopted kids feel, day after day, until time helps the new become the familiar to them. After I saw my kids repeat this "brown out" effect of over stimulation over and over again, I started making their world smaller. And the best advice I can offer anyone bringing home an older child from another country through adoption is to keep your child's world *very, very small, small, small* at first.

I wish I could say I did this, but I didn't know what I didn't know. If I could do it all over again, I would think of their orientation to their new life in concentric circles. Think of your house as the first circle. When your kids get home, even if it seems mundane, spend the first few days just taking them through your home, room by room, explaining to them how each room "works" and what its purpose is. Open cabinets and drawers, and explain what goes where. Show them how to use things and how to close drawers and how to turn on the shower.

Stay home. Don't go to church, don't go to parties, and don't go driving around. Give your kids a chance to understand and master their home before you move out to the next circle, your neighborhood.

Next, walk around the neighborhood and explain how it "works". Many children from other countries don't understand American mores, like the privacy boundary of a home. My kids have told me that in their country, if you need something, you can just go from house to house until someone has what you need or can help you. Many doors in their country don't have locks (many homes don't even have doors), so walking right in is common place.

Obviously, this approach is not acceptable or even safe in our cul-de-sac world where we may not even know many of our neighbors. Help your kids learn the spoken and unspoken rules of their new neighborhood. Ride bikes, play in your street, and just get used to your neighborhood. Then, begin taking your kids out in the car, one destination at a time, without overwhelming them.

Of course, meanwhile, you will have to keep the world from showing up at your house to "meet the kids." You probably can't avoid a big airport reception when you first arrive home, but that is OK. Your kids will be too tired to care and you will need that encouragement after the grueling journey of adoption. It's really for you, not them, anyway. But that is OK – you deserve it.

Let grandparents and aunts and friends all come out to the airport to see your new kids. Let them bring balloons and flowers and cameras and signs. Let everyone exchange hugs and rejoice.

But after that, try to stay home and snuggle the kids without too many visitors. And, for as long as you possibly can, keep your child's world *small* while his brain processing catches up with American culture. Here are some specific areas to think about:

Television: Sit back sometime and watch American television as if you have never seen it, and never lived in America. A few days before we traveled to complete our adoption, I was watching an ad for wrinkle cream during the evening news. The actress was imploring me that my life would not be worthwhile unless I could eliminate the fine lines around my eyes.

I tried to imagine how those 30 seconds would sound to my soon-to-be home kids, who come from a place where women are beautiful at all ages, and struggle most days just to survive. How could they possibly understand or integrate these seemingly bizarre messages? And wrinkle cream ads are just the tip of the iceberg for all the disturbing things your kids might see on television. Shows that seem "normal" to us might seem very violent or upsetting to older adopted children.

I learned this early one day when our eight-year-old was watching a movie that our American kids had loved at that age, but he asked me to turn it off because he was frightened. Unfortunately, there is little on television these days that is edifying or soothing or educational for adopted children.

But, be prepared to fight to keep your kids away from TV. Our adopted kids are obsessed with TV. It literally affects them like a drug. They would watch it all day, every day if we let them. They cannot modulate their consumption on their own. They zone out and sit like mannequins before it, watching anything that comes on. To manage this, we have no TV during the week, and Friday night "movie nights" where we watch a rented movie, rated G. This is almost all the TV they see right now, except for some public broadcasting that is educational. I just haven't found much else that seems to have any benefit to them.

Especially the first year that they are home in America, consider significantly limiting your children's television viewing. If your family is big on TV, it will be good for all of you...you will spend more time bonding with the new kids.

Computers: Our adopted 14 year-old is a moral, highly principled child. She has a quality of being pure and undefiled, very unlike American girls her age. She is a committed student and made the honor role her first semester in America. She always completes homework as soon as it is assigned. Unbeknownst to us, her music class assigned a project on the history of Rap music. By the time this happened, we had taught her how to use the computer for homework research, so she often would do her own assignments. Before we could intervene, her homework on rap led her online to many highly sexual and violent videos, which we did not know she could access. She did not know enough to screen her search, and we did not know enough to protect her. You can imagine our horror when we learned of this situation.

Other adopted families have told us similar stories of teens ending up in chat rooms when searching online for others with their nationality, or falling easy prey to internet predators. Even if you trust your adopted child completely, you must be *extremely* judicious in monitoring her internet use. Only allow your child to use the computer when you are home and put a secure password on the computer that you control. Help with homework at all ages, and keep the computer in a room where you are present, like the kitchen. An adopted child left alone on the internet is a recipe for many dangers.

Gifts/Clothes/Toys: When your kids first arrive home, and even before they arrive home, everyone who loves your family will want to give them gifts. Many people will be touched by your adoption story, and in America, we measure our love and blessings with shopping. No matter how hard you try to dissuade them, people will buy many gifts for your children. Sometimes, you won't even know about it. On more than one occasion, our kids have arrived at the car after church carrying gift bags from members of our congregation. The problem with this is that your kids have probably had few clothes and no toys for most of their lives. So, just coming home to a closet and a dresser is going to overwhelm them at first. They are likely not used to having choices in attire, or many things to play with besides whatever is available in the outdoors. So, an avalanche of toys and clothes is just one more thing for your child to manage and process.

One strategy that helped us in this regard was to give people lists of what our kids needed, and we wanted them to have. Don't be bashful. Make a "wish list", and send it out to friends and family in advance. Include sizes and favorite colors if you know them. Make specific suggestions, like "a soccer ball", to help people shop productively. This will go a long way to keeping your sanity and keeping you from having a closet full of things that are too overwhelming for your child.

If possible, graciously accept gifts and put them away in the attic for later. Take things out one at a time or as your child grows, instead of all at once. Resist the urge to overdo the first

Christmas or birthday at home. Pick one special gift from you, and keep it at that. In the case of my three older adopted children, I made them each a memory book of photos and keepsakes on their first birthday home, including the story of their adoption. There were plenty of other toys and gifts from friends and relatives on these birthdays, and this gift will be a treasure over their lifetime.

In the end, try to keep life as simple as possible when your kids first get home. Spend family time together doing old-fashioned, basic things, like playing cards or taking nature walks. Our kids really enjoyed that time, and to be honest, we did too.

Lesson 2

"Tinkerbelle, Tinkerbelle, Tinker All

the Way..."

(One of the many wacky versions of carols sung by our kids that first Christmas home...)

(understanding)

Since my husband and I had raised children already, we thought we were prepared for the various stages and developmental milestones that we would encounter in adopting older children. With three successfully out of the house and leading productive lives, we felt qualified to do the teenage thing all over again. To be honest, I actually love the teen years, despite all their waves of drama.

So when our adopted daughters were to be 14 and 12 by the time they came home, we felt ready. But as soon as they arrived home, nothing that worked with the other kids we had raised seemed to apply to these two, especially the twelve-year-old.

Now, I know a lot about twelve-year old girls, and I was trying to give our newly adopted daughter the same choices and level of relationship with me that my older girls would have wanted at that age. But I was failing miserably. She was sullen, confused, overwhelmed and withdrawn.

Early one morning, I was reading one of the books by the experts (those ones you really need to read that are listed at the end of this book), and I came upon a chapter that said that children can get developmentally "stuck" at the age of a major trauma. That hit me like a two-by-four. Our daughter had suffered a series of extreme traumas when she was six years old, including being run over as a pedestrian and the death of her father. It was a perfect storm of horrible events in her young, precious life. Was it possible that she was "stuck" at six in a twelve-year-old body?

Later that same day, I went to the store to buy her a new pair of pajamas, hoping that would cheer her up. She was a mystery about clothes too and did not seem to like the many "preteen" clothes that family and friends had kindly filled her closet with before her arrival. Getting dressed, especially for church, had been one of the main sources of conflict and drama between us and her. But, she needed a nightgown...so this was my chance to bless her.

I walked around the store for a while, relishing a few moments alone, and could not seem to find anything in the ladies department that I thought she would wear. There is no teen department for lingerie, so I headed over to children's as a last ditch effort before abandoning my plan altogether.

As I wandered lost in thought through the racks, suddenly there they were! Hanging on the end of a clearance rack in the kid's department was the silliest garment I have ever seen. An *enormous* pair of Tinkerbelle pajamas. You know the type...these are the kinds of PJ's you put on a toddler. They were lime green and bright pink, with sparkles and a giant Tinkerbelle on the chest, but they were huge. Of course no one had bought them...a child is not that large. God's voice inside me said "She will love these." My mind said: "Are you kidding? No self respecting twelve-year-old girl would ever put those pajamas on her body." But, the voice argued, if she really *is* six inside, it might work. This could be the test. If she likes these, the theory proves true. I looked and the jammies were marked down to almost nothing, so I risked little in buying them.

Home I went with the ginormous Tinkerbelle pajamas. I went into my daughter's room where she was usually found – withdrawn from the rest of the family.

"Honey, Mom got you some new sleeping clothes" ("pajamas" was a new word for her).

With great trepidation, I pulled the sparkly wonders from the bag.

She took one look at them and her face lit up with joy. She jumped a little happy jump and clapped her hands. She was overcome with delight. She thought they were the most wonderful gift she had ever received.

"Mum, I LOVE these" she said with a huge smile.

She wore them for the next three weeks. Constantly while not at school -- like loungewear.

After this, I got it. Yes, she might be *intellectually* twelve or *physically* twelve, but inside she was a six-year-old little girl.

I couldn't wait to tell my husband the news – the "aha" moment I needed to figure out how to parent her. Within 24 hours, we had changed our strategy and approach with her, and everything changed for the better. I told her grandmother to get her a doll for Christmas, I bought her t-shirts with bears on them, we rented all of the Disney princess movies.

Life for our girl became a wonderful opportunity to lavish her with all the things we had done for our other girls when they were little. We baked cookies and sang songs and bought coloring books. We changed our plans for her 13th birthday party, and threw her a "Princess" themed party; complete with every princess gift or game we could conjure. And our daughter just blossomed.

Once we figured this out, a lot of our expectations of her changed as well. For example, most of our kids put in their own laundry once they are pre-teens. But with this child, my husband was consistently frustrated on her laundry day. Every time it was her turn to put in her wash, the washing machine would somehow "jam" and fail to run its cycle. And he would have to reset the machine to get it to work. At first, it was a mystery.

But after the "aha" moment, well, it all made sense! Because you wouldn't let a six-year-old put in wash, would

20

you? A six-year-old would push all the buttons, dump the soap and make a mess of things. In this case, if we had not figured out she was "six" and not "twelve", we might have punished her for playing with the washing machine, thinking she was not being "responsible" like her siblings.

And if we had punished her for this washing machine fiasco, it would have just set off just another chain reaction of unhappiness on her part and ours. She would have been mystified and hurt by the punishment, and we would have been frustrated by her lack of cooperation. But, now that we understood better her other "developmental age", we just loaded the wash for her. It was a small thing that saved her and us so much headache and angst.

So you may be thinking by now that if you let your child do these "regressed" things, you are not helping him grow or make progress. Don't worry that you will keep your kid "stuck" at a regressed level if you make these adjustments. Our adopted kids are resilient sponges. Once given the chance to be every age, your child will "catch up" as he is ready.

With our daughter, within a few short months, the dolls that she so desperately wanted and played with had already been given away – by her—to her younger friends. Once she had the chance to play with dolls, she was able to move on. She told me,

"Mum, I don't need these any more. I want to play with older things now."

So, if your teenage son lost his mother when he was eight, and now he is not fitting in with the boys in the neighborhood and driving you crazy, maybe buy him some Legos. Sit with him at the kitchen table and build cool things with him. Teach him English using comic books instead of his textbooks. Take him to a play ground on a rainy day when there aren't small kids around, and climb around with him. In whatever way you can, take him back through all the boy stuff that he missed while he was in a fog of grief, and give him a chance to be a superhero to you. And don't worry about one bit of it. He will be a responsible young man soon, and you will be very proud.

Lesson 3

"Will There Be Chicken In America?"

(eating)

One of the most challenging things about older child adoption is food issues. Sadly, most orphaned kids have experienced chronic hunger of one form or another, some for many years. In the case of our children, all their years in the orphanage had been defined by two meals per day of posho, a sticky porridge made with corn flour.

Imagine eating nothing but grits for one full week. No butter or salt, just grits. Now imagine eating only grits for a month. How about for a year? Many orphaned children experience months if not years of extreme hunger and malnourishment, consuming institutional orphanage diets designed to fill hungry bellies but not offer much more.

Our kids were served posho and beans almost every day for years. On Christmas and Easter (they were raised in a Christian orphanage), they got one piece of chicken. One day while I was unloading a big bag of oranges from the grocery store, my daughter commented "Before we came here, it could be a year before I could eat one orange."

As you might imagine then, coming to America -- where the biggest child health epidemic is obesity -- would be not only be shocking but confusing. In our culture, food is *everywhere*. We eat three times a day, plus snacks. We eat in our cars, our offices, while shopping and even churches now

24

have coffee bars and cafes, as we can't seem to go any length of time without putting something in our mouths.

I knew my kids were eating posho and porridge in the orphanage, but I was unprepared for how completely *obsessed* with food my children would be as a result of being deprived so long.

I will never forget the first meal we ate with our children on the trip we took to complete their adoption. We were at a small café in the town near their village, and at the end of the simple meal (they ordered...chicken), our son asked my husband if there was ice cream at that restaurant and could he have some? Of course my husband responded,

"Ice cream for everyone!"

Shyness and fear immediately dissolved into huge smiles on all the children's faces – for we were to learn that they had dreamed of having parents who could buy them ice cream.

In fact, we later learned that this went even deeper. One of their special memories of their deceased father was of him buying them an ice cream at the end of a day. In their little hearts, ice cream was a symbol of love and happiness and being cared for. One of the children even later told us,

"When Dad bought us that ice cream, we knew that God had given us back another father like the one we had lost."

What an incredible example of the power of food in our feelings of security!

We saw this play out in all three of the children, but especially in one. She admitted to us that when she was ten-years old, she had actually planned to take her own life because she was "tired of being so hungry."

Just a small girl, she managed to get a few coins and purchased a vial of rat poison. She walked a long way to get a cup of water to mix up the rat poison (water was not readily available where she lived), and then she made the potion that was to end her life.

Sitting before it, she prayed to God to forgive her for what she was about to do. As she reached for the cup, she heard someone call her name, startled, and knocked the cup over. Many weeks of planning had gone into getting the money for the poison, so her plan was foiled. I thank God every day that this plan was not completed!

This child uses food as a comfort and reassurance, as do many of us. Six months before her adoption took place (but after we were already in communication with the children), she aged out of the orphanage and we sent her to live with some U.S. missionaries until we could come for her. It was during this time that she began overeating. Although she was obedient, intelligent and helpful in every other way with these hosts, she was eating way more than her small body needed. By the time we came for her, she had already started gaining weight at an alarming rate. This continued for several months after we got home, as she reveled in having plenty to eat.

Conversely, her sister was afraid to try any American foods and refused most of what she was offered for weeks and months after coming home. She lived on rice, beans and of course, chicken.

As a busy Mom, I soon came to realize my reliance on fast, easy "kid food" to efficiently feed my family was a thing of the past (cereal, pizza, grilled cheese -- all alien foods of no use to me in feeding the new kids.) Even sandwiches were initially off the menu -- they wanted no part of them. I eventually got them to cave into peanut butter sandwiches in their lunch sack, but lunch meat and cheese were snubbed at first!

So here we were with one child who was eating too much of everything and two who wouldn't eat, along with our other kids who were used to having a hearty American supper each night. This made meal times stressful at best.

In addition, the new kids were consumed with worrying about food in general. At each meal, they would begin asking about the *next* meal before we even finished eating at the table. What was the next meal? When would it be? What time would we have it? How much food would there be? Despite our huge pantry stocked from a discount grocery warehouse, the children were *always* worried that we were going to *run out of food*.

Even months after we had been home, our youngest still worried daily. When we would patiently reassure him that we could always go shopping if we ran out of something, he revealed that he was afraid we would "not have enough money" when the supply ran out. Scarcity of all kind, extreme poverty and lack were such an imbedded part of his consciousness that he could not grasp the idea that we have *always* had enough money for food and *never* missed a meal.

Over time, we eventually found our way through this maze of fears and emotions and settled into a pattern of comfortably eating as a family, but it took some time.

One thing that I finally did in exasperation was to create and post on the refrigerator a weekly menu. On Monday, chicken, potatoes and greens, on Tuesday, fish, rice and beans, on Wednesday, spaghetti, etc. Next week -- same menu. Although this seems mundane and like organizational overkill, it made a huge difference in the amount of anxiety around eating for my kids. If Tuesday was fish and rice, on Monday they could check and see that these items were already in stock at home waiting for Tuesday. And somehow this hugely reassured them and took away ninety percent of the questions and worrying.

Additionally, it gave us all a chance to come up with meals and ingredients that everyone could like and agree upon, so there could be no refusing at mealtime. Finally, it greatly simplified grocery shopping. While the rest of the family had to sacrifice a little in variety, the predictability of the same breakfast (eggs) and lunch (peanut butter sandwich) and seven dinner choices was the amount of simplicity that the new kids needed physically and emotionally at first.

I have heard of many older adopted children that have nutritional or eating issues of one kind or another at first, so your child likely will as well. Just take your time getting her acclimated and before you know it, she will be asking for new things and happily helping you in the kitchen!

Lesson 4

"I Need a Pumpkin"

(speaking)

One day a precious friend, who is from the same country as our three recently adopted children, came to have dinner with the family. At the end of the evening as she prepared to leave, I called upstairs to the kids who were getting ready for bed.

"Children, would you like to come say goodbye to your Auntie?"

The answer I got from the top of the stairs,

"No thanks."

I stood there with my cheeks burning, thoroughly embarrassed. I was sure that my friend thought I was terrible mother and had done a terrible job of teaching these children their manners.

But, my friend smiled kindly at me and gently explained that the children were not being rude. In fact, she told me that "would" is one of the hardest words for them to learn. It is rarely used in their language and never used when addressing children. In her culture, a child is always given direct, specific commands by adults. Children have few if any rights and they are basically told what to do and when to do it with few pleasantries or qualifiers. "Eat your food". "Go to bed." "Scrub the floor." "Come kiss your auntie goodbye."

My style of addressing them, saying things like "would you like to say goodbye" or "would you like to come to dinner" was actually confusing to them, because according to her they did not understand this was really a directive, not a question. She let me know that one of the hardest things for her to overcome when she immigrated was that Americans speak too indirectly in our attempts to be polite.

Well, that just cleared up a myriad of confusion for me! When the kids first arrived, my husband especially had many issues with the way the children spoke to him and me. He was very concerned that they were being disrespectful in their tone and language toward us.

Instead of saying,

"Mom, would you please get me some shampoo?"

My children would say,

"Mum, you need to buy me shampoo" with a brisk tone.

I came to realize that this was just a difference in cultural communication and not meant to be any disrespect at all on their parts. They were struggling just to communicate in English so the nuances and subtleties of manners were beyond what they could manage or even understand at the time.

In fact, I have learned that many of the words that we commonly use are not even translatable in their language. And, of course the syntax and sentence structure is very different as well.

This led to a season of patience and hilarity as we all got used to each other's language and manner of speaking. We really had no appreciation for how many idioms there are in English, or how bizarre some of them are, until we heard them through our kid's ears.

We also came to appreciate that learning English in school in another country was not the same as being able to speak conversational English in America. And, Americans are not without our own ignorance or misunderstanding in trying to teach adopted kids English.

For example, in our first meeting with our youngest child's English as a Second Language (ESL) teacher at his elementary school, she was reviewing test results with us and earnestly explained that she was surprised our son had not known the words "blond" or "mitten" as those would be considered basic to a child with his English level.

Really?

We tried to explain to her patiently, without sounding incredulous, that he had just arrived from an *East African tropical country* where no one was blond or wore mittens! One would think that this would have been self-explanatory to the teacher, as she knew his country of origin, but apparently not!

36

So don't assume that people relating with your child will really have any clue about where they came from, where that country is on a map and what that might mean for their communication abilities.

And, you will also have to keep in mind that when your child is learning English, words that sound similar can be confusing. Sometimes you have to work hard as a parent to keep a straight face when your child makes word choice errors like:

pumpkin for napkin

sunscream for sunscreen

practice spoon for plastic spoon

coupon for tampon

sweet belt for seat belt

upsad for upset

leray race for relay race

burger and flies for...well, you know!

And if that isn't enough, one of the most confusing things in our house is that there are two letters in my children's native language that are pronounced just like two other letters in our language. In their language, the letter "r" is pronounced like "l", and vice versa. So, when they are talking, any word with an "l" sound ends up with an "r" in it. For example, "milk" is said "mirik".

This may not seem like a big deal, but the possibilities become endless. Consider that Nathan is always asking to "pray" with his friends when he wants to "play" and "play" before bed when he wants to "pray." It goes on and on like this so we always have to clarify to be sure we understand each other.

The most disastrous example of this came one morning when he had been suffering from a bad head cold for several days. I was downstairs drinking coffee and reading my Bible early one morning when I heard his bedroom door fly open. (This was not that unusual since Nathan is a very exuberant boy and always gets up in the morning with a loud bump.)

"Mum" he shouted down the stairs, "I'm breathing."

"That's great honey" I replied calmly, thinking that his head cold was better and he was happy to be breathing clearly again.

"But Mum!" he shouts with more urgency,

"I'm breathing!!!"

"Yes honey, I heard you. That's great. I am glad you are feeling better" I say and return to my reading.

Finally, I hear him trying to come down the stairs awkwardly because his hands were over his face.

"Mum!" he says with great exasperation.

"I'm breathing, I'm breathing!!!!!"

Finally I looked up from my book long enough to see that he has a gushing bloody nose and was dripping blood all over the stairs! He meant "bleeding" but he said "breeding" and I heard "breathing."

Yikes! It's a wonder we manage to communicate at all!

One last thing regarding communication that adds to the confusion is the varying styles of non-verbal communication in different cultures. Each culture has its own ways that people greet each other and also spoken or unspoken social mores for addressing those of various statures.

For example, it is well known that the Japanese bow when greeting someone and that shaking hands would be seen as a great affront in their culture. Well, keep in mind that your older adopted child will bring with her the mores of her culture, particularly as it relates to addressing new people and those in authority.

One of the issues I had with my kids when they first got home is that every time I tried to teach them or correct them, they would not look at me. The lack of eye contact from them was driving me crazy. I had always been taught that one of the first rules of parenting was to make eye contact with your child -- especially when you are trying to teach them something or correct them. Books even tell you to "get down on the child's level" so you can look them in the eye. Unless someone is looking at me, I feel like I am not really connecting with him, and he is not really hearing me.

So you can imagine my frustration when my kids would look down at the floor every time I had something important to say to them.

Then I was talking one day with a friend who has children that were adopted from the same part of the world, and she reminded me of the fact that in our children's native culture, it is forbidden for a child to look an adult in the eyes. Oh man...I had missed that completely! So, all those times I thought they were *disrespecting* me; they were actually *respecting* me in their minds! Talk about a lack of communication!

As you learn to talk with your kids, just take your time. Don't assume the worst. And try to remember that most of communication comes from the heart not the lips. If you don't believe me, I offer as an example the first letter I received from Nathan, age 7, one month after he was adopted. It may not be correct English, but I understood it perfectly.

Nathan Tucker. 12-16-10.

Dear Mom

Dear mom I love You our ano You orp aser oroq
love I love our mom ore soro

Dear mom I need You Bur you neey Ber

Mom I love our mom 200 an 100

Mom Do you love our You nur benwor

And I love You. Do You love our ben

Ort I love You. love Nathan. your daughter.

Lesson 5

It's Not What You Think

(listening)

A local reporter learned of our plans to adopt, and followed our family's story over the eighteen months of our adoption process. Once the children arrived home, the feature article ran on Christmas day, with full color photos, on the front page of our regional newspaper. I had mixed feelings about all that, as I wondered how my children would feel about their loss and abandonment being portrayed to the entire world in such a public way.

We planned to wait for a few days after Christmas to tell them about the article because we were not sure what their reaction would be. But soon we had no choice because when the children returned to school after the winter break, their friends mentioned seeing it. So that evening in early January, we showed them the story and let them read it.

After reading the article, we all gathered in the living room for our nightly time of sharing and prayer. One of our newly adopted daughters sat in her usual spot, but she had a sour look on her face. She was not smiling, not making eye contact, and looking very angry. As others in the family were sharing, my thoughts were racing...what had I done?! I was so afraid that the article had embarrassed or hurt her in some way. I was afraid she felt ashamed. I feared I had exploited her pain. I feared that she would never forgive me and resent me for sensationalizing her story in an effort to encourage others to adopt.

Finally I could take it no longer. In the middle of the family devotional, I burst out and asked her pointedly,

"Honey, are you alright? I am so sorry. Tell me what you are feeling? Is it the article? Tell me what is bothering you so much!"

She answered,

"Oh Mum. I love the article. It's just that right before we sat down together, Nathan hit me in the face with the couch pillow, and I am really mad at him."

So there it was. All my fears and parental insecurities and self-doubt and anxiety and everything I had been obsessed with was completely and totally off base. It all came down to a simple bonk in the face by a little brother with a throw pillow!

And I remember in that moment thinking: *with these new kids, it's never what I think it is.*

I wish I could remember and share with you all the times this has happened, but suffice it to say that with our older adopted children, it happens a lot.

We see the world through our lens, with our script, with our set of cultural expectations or psychological issues, and we interpret our children's actions and emotions through that lens. But so often with older children from another place, we can be totally off-case in our interpretation of what is happening. Or, what is really going on is so far outside our expectation or understanding that we don't know where to begin.

45

A far more serious example of this happened just a few weeks later. The same child was sullen for days, sinking into a dark place that I did not seem to be able to penetrate. She was acting uncharacteristically angry and withdrawn, refusing to communicate with the rest of the family. I finally corner her in her room, shut the door, and said

"Honey, you must tell me what is wrong."

What ensued was a two hour verbal "take down." She admitted something was wrong, but would not tell me what it was. She was weeping and in despair. I finally got her to admit that something bad had happened to her in the past, but she would not reveal it.

We finally arrived at the place in the conversation where she said she would allow me to *guess* what happened to her, and she would answer "yes" or "no" to my questions.

For half an hour, I guessed everything a mother would never want to speak. I guessed every horrible act imaginable. To which all the answers were "no." On and on I guessed until I had ruled out any act by any person I could name. I ran out of guesses, and we just sat there on the edge of the bed, drying her tears. I was stumped.

I knew this was a critical moment for us. She clearly had a huge burden, and I couldn't help her if I didn't know what it was. After about another thirty minutes of cajoling, she finally revealed her torment.

Here is the story. Apparently, in her culture, it is customary to ask someone to tend your grave after your death. This is considered to be a great honor. When she was a small child, my daughter was asked by the sister of her father to tend her grave after her death. It was a very unusual request for a small child, and interpreted by the family at the time as a great recognition of her maturity and responsibility.

The aunt died soon thereafter, and my small child actually tended the grave. Later when she went to live in the orphanage, she could no longer attend to this duty. She said that since that time, she had been plagued with horrible nightmares of this deceased woman coming to her in the night with a large knife, trying to kill her. These terrifying dreams followed her to America and worsened since the adoption. She believed the spirit of this woman was angry with her and that she would be haunted endlessly.

Well, of all the terrible things I could imagine had befallen my little girl, being haunted by the ghost of her dead aunt was not one of them! Once again, I did not have the cultural context to know what I could not know. Thankfully, once this was out in the open, she and I were able to talk through it and pray for her to be released from these dreams. She has not had another one since, and I am so grateful that I took the time to really understand what was troubling her.

The lesson for me in both these examples is that you cannot over-communicate when it comes to older adopted children. It makes sense that you have missed years of their experiences, and that you should take time to learn all you can, but once we find ourselves overwhelmed with children, jobs and family schedules, our good intentions of spending quality time with each child can lose its place as a priority among all the other demands of family life.

I needed this reminder that my child had years of memories and experiences, and I was going to have to make a real effort to get to know her and hear her stories if I was going to be an effective parent for her.

My friend has three children that were adopted from Ethiopia, and she taught me to be prepared at any time to "drop what I am doing" and listen. She said the stories often come at "safe" times that remind the child of home and family, like bedtime, and when one is in the kitchen cooking. So, she encouraged me to be ready to turn off the stove while preparing dinner, or relax a bedtime, if it meant my child was ready to share about her life.

I must confess I have not followed this advice to the degree I wish I had, but I remain committed to take the time to hear every story so that I can know each of my kids intimately.

Lesson 6

The "M-Word"

(bonding)

My husband affectionately calls it the "M-Word" because it has become so overused in our house, it is almost an annoyance. My adopted children call my name, "Mum" (as they say it with their accent), *hundreds* of times per day. That is not an exaggeration. It begins the second they wake up in the morning, see me or know I am in the house. And it goes on all day.

Our little boy is the first one up every morning. If I manage to get up ahead of him to have a little time for coffee and prayer, I know the first word I will hear as soon as he discovers me is "Mum." He doesn't say "Good Morning;" he doesn't say "Hi;" He says "Mum."

All three of the newly adopted kids do this. If we are all in the kitchen together, everyone will be addressing me at once.

"Mum, Mum, Mum."

Each of them competes to see who I will attend to first.

For example, while cooking dinner, it goes like this:

"Mum, how should I cut this?"

"Mum, look at how I set the table."

"Mum, what does this mean?"

"Mum, where is the cup?"

"Mum, how do I open this?"

"Mum, do you like this picture?"

"Mum, did you see my teacher's note?"

"Mum, what should I do now?"

If I try to leave the room, as I begin to walk away, each will say "Mum" almost in a small panic. Then, they will think of something to ask me because what they really want is for me to not leave the room.

I can't describe fully how completely overwhelming this behavior was at first when the children came home. It was relentless. They were so afraid to be left. They got anxious if I went to the store, for example. Running out to get milk meant a big discussion.

"Where are you going?"

"How long would you be gone?"

"What time will you come back?"

"What should we do while you are gone?"

This happens even when Dad is home and loving and attentive. One child confessed to me one time,

"Mum, I hate it when you sleep."

For the first several months after the children came home, I would literally brace myself before getting up in the morning or coming into the house if I had been out.

"God, please give me the strength and patience to meet their every need," I would pray to myself.

I understood the source of this behavior, and I knew the only way past it was *through* it. But it was hard - very hard. Until the children became convinced that they could count on me, I had to be there for them.

It was seven months before I finally broke under the demands. One busy Saturday morning I had the whole crew doing chores with me. I was rushing around the house multi-tasking. As I was carrying laundry and trying to complete some cleaning task, Ruth calls to me:

"Mum, come and see how I cleaned the tub."

But, my arms were full of laundry and I was under a time crunch and headed in the other direction to do something.

"I am busy" I said to her.

It was like a bomb dropped. She slumped her head and slunk away with her shoulders drooping.

Immediately, I began feeling guilty. I must be the worst mother in the world. Did I let her down? Would she still trust me? And later that day, don't you just know she brought it back up to me.

"Mum, today you said you were too busy to see what I had done."

But thankfully I stood my ground. I told her I appreciated what she had done, but I had something else that needed my time at that moment. At some point, you will have to set this boundary with your child, but it will be a balancing act.

So, as I am writing this now, our little boy finds me.

"Mum, what are you doing?"

"I am doing some work, son."

"Mum, do you want to play with me?"

"I am busy right now, son."

Then, he goes in for the clincher...he looks up at me with those giant eyes and says:

"Mum, you need a blake." (see Chapter 4 if you don't get it...)

I can't resist him. I mean, could you resist this?

It goes without saying that orphaned children have not had their needs met for parental love. But it is hard to understand what that will really mean or how it will express itself until you experience it. And, it will take different forms in different children – even within the same sibling group.

Older children might express this by constantly asking you for things, even things they can do for themselves. One of my teen daughters comes to me with every little scratch and bump, wanting me to make a fuss over it.

"Mum, I cut my finger with paper. Will you kiss it?"

I think to myself, "Why doesn't she just get a Band-aid and keep doing her homework?" But then I realize that when she was a little girl, nobody kissed her skinned knees or hugged her when she fell down. She lived at the orphanage since age four. Now at fourteen, she still has the need for a Mommy to kiss her injury and give her attention. So I try to be patient and fill that need.

I have a friend who told me that her newly adopted 15-year-old son was running her ragged. He was constantly asking her to do things for him that he could and should do himself: make his bed, fix his lunch, wake him for school (even though he had an alarm clock), drive him to school (even though he could take the bus).

This was from a boy who was living on his own and taking care of himself completely prior to his adoption! But on and on he put these demands on her until she was exhausted by them.

Most teens are fighting for independence, and we are lucky if we can get them to even interact with us. But this young man was nowhere near that developmental milestone. Having lived without parents most of his life, he needed to "catch up" by first experiencing the doting love of mother.

Even though he had been living on his own and surviving, emotionally he was not ready to move to independence. Now that he had mother, he wanted the reassurance built by a child's total dependence on a parent.

This same issue will be apparent with physical boundaries and affection. Just as your children may constantly want your attention, they many also have an intense need for physical contact. It breaks my heart to think about my kids going to bed night after night in the orphanage without someone to kiss them goodnight and give them a hug.

Now that they are part of our family, I see the scars of this neglect in them, but it is not the same in each child. One child is a sponge for physical touch, even beyond what is appropriate for her age. She wants hugs all day every day. She wants to hold my hand while we watch TV. She is constantly touching me.

Her sister, on the other hand, resists touch entirely. She is uncomfortable with affection and avoids it. Initially, she did not want to be hugged by either me or my husband *at all*. Having read all the good books on this issue of attachment with younger children, we tried to give her time and space to become comfortable. Slowly, very slowly, she would let us embrace her. Now, she gives and receives hugs and love, but it was definitely a process.

So I can't tell you exactly what you will encounter. But I can tell you that you are probably in for an intense game of emotional cat and mouse if you adopt an older child. You will need lots of patience and grace for yourself and that child, and lots of support from your spouse or other parents.

Be patient. Your kids *will* bond with you...it's what they want most in the world. You just might take a road to get there that is not one you expected.

Lesson 7

"Oh, You Are My Mother"

(disciplining)

One of the more difficult aspects of older child adoption is discipline. Anyone who has been through the adoption process has endured the standard questions asked by a social worker during the Home Study process. (For those of you who have not yet adopted, the Home Study is required in any adoption. A social worker conducts a series of visits with you and your family, and produces a report on your suitability for adoption for the court proceedings.)

Just like there are standard job interview questions, there are standard Home Study questions, and discipline is always a topic. You will be asked some iteration of:

"What are your methods of disciplining children?"

"Do you believe in spanking or corporal punishment?"

"How will you discipline your adopted child?"

Hopefully having answered each of these questions to the best of your knowledge and with whatever are the "politically correct" attitudes toward punishment, you passed your Home Study with flying colors. But let me tell you, everything you know or think about disciplining children, when it comes to older child adoption, you can just throw what you think right out the window!

The lesson I have learned is that discipline is an issue that is largely, almost entirely driven by culture. So much so that what is a punishment in one culture might not even seem like a punishment in another. And something that makes perfect sense in America might seem completely bizarre and hurtful to a child from another country.

The other thing that makes disciplining the older adopted child so challenging is you don't know the background of your child. You probably won't know many small or even significant traumas they experienced, or injuries they sustained, or a million other little things that are the lore of a lifetime. And so many of the things you may find "disobedient" might be related to a trauma or fear or confusion and, had you parented that child from birth, you would understand that behavior.

In addition, when your child first comes home, you will not yet know what "makes them tick." And, as any seasoned parent knows, knowing what makes a particular child tick is the key to effective discipline!

When your older adopted child arrives as a mostly grown human being, there is no time for figuring all this stuff out. And there WILL be discipline issues. If you have any fantasies that your older adopted child will be so appreciative of "what you have done for him" that he will just swoon at your every request, you need to throw away those fantasies right now.

Take heart, we all think that during the pre-adoption wait. We all assume that these kids are old enough to understand the enormous commitment we have made to adopt them, look at the huge change in their circumstances before and after adoption, and think we are the greatest parents on

Earth. But, it doesn't really pan out that way. (more about this in Lesson 8).

At the end of the day, they are still just kids. And their lack of parenting *before* adoption, coupled with their own fantasies *about* adoption, means you are going to be on a rocky road, at least initially.

So, the first thing to evaluate is what, if any, parenting has your child experienced. If your child lived in an institution for an extended period of time, it is important that you ask her about the rules at that place and how discipline was handled. This will go a long way to helping you understand what *her* understanding of discipline might be.

In the case of our three children, discipline at their orphanage meant one thing and one thing only – "beating." Now, this is the word they used, and another example of the importance of understanding language. In their language, "beating" is the equivalent to "spanking" and it is pretty much applied at any age up to adulthood.

There was a staff member at this orphanage of six-hundred children whose job it was to maintain order, and he literally walked around with a paddle. Any infraction was met with a paddling, more for more serious disobedience.

Even academic performance was managed in this way. One day I was struggling to help Ruth with her multiplication tables, and she informed me that she had been paddled for not knowing them at the orphanage. Now why didn't I think of that?! That would have saved me so much time making flashcards (I am kidding here folks).

For my kids, the *only* form of punishment that they understood was having a piece of wood applied to their backside.

And we did need to discipline them because older adopted children will test you. They will test you for many, many reasons, but here are just a few. Your child will test you because:

- o He has never known parents or hasn't had them in a long time.

- o He doesn't understand that relating in a family is not the same as surviving in an institution.

- o He doesn't understand the meaning or importance of the rules of your home.

- o He isn't sure you really want him so he wants to see just how much you will take.

- o He learned at the orphanage to lie, cheat, manipulate or connive just to get enough food and survive.

- o He doesn't understand that his behavior hurts you personally because no one cares if you act badly in foster care.

- o He has been on his own so long as a child head-of-household that he is not accustomed to coming under your authority.

- o He is considered "grown" or adult in his country and he can't understand why he needs parents to control his decisions.

- o He is troubled by darkness from his past, and he is still confused about being in a safe place.

o   He has been hurt so much already that his heart is afraid to trust.

I am sure I could keep going with this list, but you get the point. So be prepared to be tested, and to spend some time figuring out what form of discipline will work for your adopted child.

Some of the common methods for discipline in America are spanking, time-out, being "grounded", taking away toys or favorite objects, being sent to one's room or being given extra chores.

We have tried each of these with our adopted kids, with surprising results.

A few days after our kids arrived home, I took them on a Wal-Mart outing to shop for clothes. This turned out to be a total disaster. (I did not yet know the "Keep it Small" lesson and never should have tried to manage all three of them by myself in a store that large so early in their transition.)

Two of the children wandered off in the store while I was in the dressing room struggling with a third. When I discovered they were gone, they were nowhere to be found. With terror, I searched the entire mega-store in panic until I found them. And when I did, I was furious.

"Never, ever, ever leave Mommy without telling me! I didn't know where you were. Something could have happened to you. Someone could have taken you!"

(They looked at me totally perplexed on that one.)

"But Mum, we were just looking at everything."

As soon as we got home, I sent the two wanderers off to their room as a punishment.

Now, I had read in books that "time-out" is not to be used with young adopted children because it reminds them of abandonment. But, I really didn't expect the same response from two young teens. How wrong I was.

Little did I know being sent to their room was the most awful punishment I could have leveraged on them that day.

When I let them out of their room an hour later, they were frantic. One had actually plotted how she might escape out the second-story window using a rope of sheets. These kids had never in their entire lives been confined in any way.

Even though their new room was a source of great joy when they chose to be in it, being forced to stay in it with the door shut completely *freaked them out.* They felt rejected, they thought I didn't love them, and they couldn't believe I would discipline them so "severely." This from children who were paddled in the orphanage!

This hour in their room set our relationship back for days. They were convinced that I must not love them one bit if I "sent them away."

So, the next time punishment was needed, we thought we would "ground" them or take some object away. But, at this early stage in the game, my kids had little that could be removed. They didn't have friends yet, weren't watching TV or using the phone and had few toys. And besides…we were trying to teach them to enjoy their new things. Taking away something had little impact. They had lived with almost nothing most of their lives and did not treasure these things as American kids do.

And assigning extra chores was like giving them a gift. My Ugandan children love doing chores around the house. It is a great source of esteem for them. They will do any task happily.

We ran out of options realizing these approaches weren't impactful.

That left us only one method to consider...spanking.

I rarely if ever spanked my other kids. In fact, the one time I tried it with Olivia when she was three, she hit me back!

And the last thing I wanted to do was strike a child that I was trying so hard to bond with. So, we were stumped.

Right about that time, my friend with three kids from Ethiopia told me an amazing story.

Her middle adopted child is high-spirited. She is an emotional child who can be a bit of a drama queen. When she was first adopted with her siblings, she was the one who had the hardest time settling into her new family. The children did not speak English fluently, so that added to the confusion.

Every time this little girl got upset about something, she became emotional and tried to run out of the house.

Now my friend is one of the sweetest, most laid-back Moms ever. I can't imagine her losing her temper or striking her child. But apparently, one day after chasing this child down the street on one of her "escapes", my girlfriend lost her cool and when she reached her, she grabbed her up and gave her a hearty whack on the bottom.

The little girl looked up at her and said,

"Oh, you are my mother!"

No kidding.

In her culture, a parent spanks a child and so when she received the spanking, she somehow understood on a much more intuitive level that she really had a new mom.

By now you know where this is going.

Yup, we have a wooden spoon. We have not used it on the fourteen year old, but it has been employed a few times on the little one, and one very memorable time on the twelve-year old who was trying to sneak out the front door in the dark one night after she had been sent to bed.

And guess what? It works great. Just the threat of the spoon is all it took to get our kids to respect our authority. We finally figured out that corporal punishment was the symbol of parental authority that they understood and so that was the type of authority we needed to use to help them respect us as their parents.

By now, you may be thinking we are cruel, awful parents. I promise you, we aren't. We shower our children with love and affection. We tell them every day that we love them. We hug them and hold their hands and tell them they are special. Nathan and I have a little game that he gets "100 kisses" from me every day.

But we also need them to know that we are the final authority in their lives now. Older adopted children may have never had anyone to protect them and advocate for them. Another adoptive Mom I know has to tell her adopted late teen daughter almost daily,

"My job is to keep you safe."

You may be forced to reconsider what worked in parenting your other children and adapt your style to fit the culture or history of your adopted child. It won't kill you. Your child has had to adapt to thousands of things to assimilate into your world. This is one thing you can do for her to let her know that you *really are her mother.*

Lesson 8

"I Thought We Would Ride In A Limo"

(expecting)

Expectations are a funny thing. We create them for ourselves, but they are often the source of our greatest disappointments.

If you are considering adopting, in the process of adopting, or even already adopted a child years ago, chances are there are expectations involved.

You probably have expectations for your adopted child. You may expect her to be a certain way, or like everything you like, or believe everything you believe. You may expect him to treat you a certain way or behave a certain way or develop a certain way. You may expect your child to love and adore you for all you have done. You may expect a lot of things.

Forget about it.

Parenting, especially parenting a child not of your womb, is a crap shoot at worst and a divine mystery at best. Your adopted child will be an unknown quantity with personality traits and quirks and fears and desires that you can't predict.

Wherever you are in the adoption journey, I suggest for your own well-being that you write down all your expectations on a piece of paper -- get it all out of your system -- and then rip up that piece of paper and throw it away. Open your heart to receive God's plan for your life and for your child's. Because the ironic thing is, God might just EXCEED your expectations.

I read a hilarious quote one time that said,

"Adoption is not for wimps."

Now THAT is brilliant.

If you are the kind of person who needs to control everything or predict everything or decide everything, adoption is going to make you very, very unhappy. It's a faith journey.

But if you are the kind of person who loves people, who is fascinated with relationships, who believes that everyone has value, then you will love being an adoptive parent. And if you are blessed enough to be given the awesome gift of raising a child that was once an orphan, you are likely to find it the most rewarding experience of your life. A neighbor of mine with two kids from Russia said to me before my kids got home,

"It will be the hardest thing you ever do, and it will be the best thing you ever do."

She was so right.

Much more important in the lesson of expectations was not getting rid of *my* expectations, but understanding my child's.

It didn't take me long to figure out that my kids had a lot of expectations about adoption, families and America that were not grounded in any truth.

When a child in an orphanage is selected for adoption, a great fable begins in which all of the child's friends tell him every myth they have ever heard about the U.S. Even adults in the institution may say ridiculous things to your child so he will "go along" with the adoption. Things like,

"When you get your new parents, you can ask them for anything you want, and they will give it to you."

Hmmm.

I am blessed to be surrounded by a Christian community that has embraced older child adoption, so I have the benefit of knowing many amazing children that have been adopted after the age of 5.

Along the way in writing this book, I interviewed my kids and their adopted friends about what were their expectations before adoption and what were the most surprising things to them after being adopted. What I heard reads like a bad fantasy novel.

"I thought we would meet President Obama."

"I thought we would eat ice cream every day."

"I thought I would have my own room with a television in it."

"I thought we would always be shopping."

"I thought children were not punished in America."

"I thought there were only white people in America."

"I didn't think there were thieves in America."

"I thought I would not have to do chores."

"I thought I would live next door to all the other children who had been adopted from my orphanage."

"I was surprised at how badly the children act in school here."

"I did not think there were poor or homeless people in America."

"I thought I would be able to tell who is Haitian, who is African and who is American, but all black kids look the same to me here."

"I thought everyone had huge families with lots of children."

"I thought the radio station I listened to in the orphanage would be on my radio in America."

"I thought we would only go to school when we felt like it."

"I thought I could eat candy at every meal."

"I thought we would know movie stars."

"I thought I could get anything I wanted."

"I thought each person in the family had a car."

"I thought I would have hundreds of toys."

"I thought I would never have any more problems."

"I thought my new parents would never get mad at me."

It doesn't take a genius to figure out that if this is all the stuff our kids were told or thought before adoption, reality could end up being a huge disappointment!

I think my adopted kids thought their new life would be a lot like OZ. So I can only imagine their dismay when they were faced with sharing and homework and no TV during the week and a mother who was not least bit like the Good Witch Glenda.

But thankfully, not everything I heard involved disappointment. There were many, many things that turned out to be so much more wonderful in adoption than these kids could even fathom.

To sum those up, I want to share one story that touched my heart deeply. A young lady who was adopted at the age of 16 told me this.

"The most surprising thing to me about my adoption was how much my parents love me. When I was a little girl in the orphanage, we watched a movie in which the parents came into the girl's room at night, tucked her in, and called her princess. When I was chosen to be adopted, all the girls at the orphanage told me that my life would be like that movie, but I did not believe it. I thought that I was much too old now and that I would never have a chance to be loved by parents in that way.

But after my sister and I got home, every night when we went to bed, my parents would come in my room. And they would tuck me in. And they would call me princess. I still can't believe they would love me that much even though I am already

grown."

Lesson 9

"My Dream Has Died"

(overcoming)

One of the joys of older child adoption is celebrating the first birthdays as a family with your children. Many adoptive children have never had a birthday party. That first birthday home with you is a huge milestone and is met with great anticipation.

Our little boy was seven years old when he came home. He had never had a birthday party in his life. In fact, he did not know his age or his actual birth date until we adopted him. In his culture, there is no time for such concerns as daily survival consumes everyone's lives.

About six months after his adoption, Nathan was due to
have a birthday to turn eight years old. By this time, his sister
had had her Princess celebration, and he had been invited to
the party of a neighborhood boy as well. So, he knew that
birthday parties meant cake, presents and fun! He was VERY
excited about the idea of having a party, and asked about it for
months before the date. He asked a million questions, made
lists of the friends he wanted to invite, talked for months about
what would be played at the party. The final countdown was at
least sixty days long!

But as the time for the party started to draw near,
suddenly I noticed his excitement waning. One day we were
alone in the car and he began questioning me about the cost of
birthday parties.

"Does it cost money to get a cake?"

"Is it a lot of money for the presents?"

"How much money did my friend's birthday cost?"

I kept trying to dodge these questions and reassure him
that my husband and I had enough money for his birthday

celebration and that he did not need to be concerned about it. But he just frowned and looked unhappy. We rode for a few miles in silence and then he spoke up again.

"Mum, I am going to tell you the truth."

"OK, son, what is the truth?"

"Mum, I don't want a birthday party. I want you to take that money and send it to my family in Uganda."

It was like a sucker punch in my gut. I knew that Nathan had dreamed about and looked forward to his birthday party for months. But now, he wanted to give it all up in the hopes that his family left behind might have some much needed resources. It was too difficult for him to think about all that attention and money spent on him when he knew others suffered. I could not believe I was hearing this from a tiny boy not yet eight years old!

I was able to work it through with him and rest assured that we did have that birthday party.

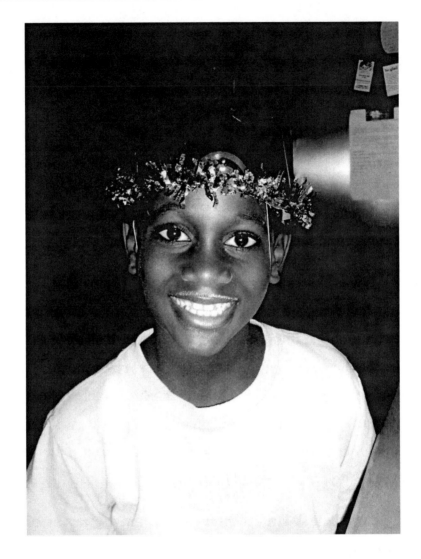

"Survivor" guilt is a serious issue in older child adoption, and one which you will likely face. I was not prepared for how deep this would go, and how much it would haunt my children. Almost weekly, I am faced with some conversation or some issue in which the children have trouble accepting the blessings of their new life in lieu of what they know others are still suffering.

We have a family tradition of having an evening devotional with our kids. We have enjoyed this activity for many years. It's nothing really formal – we gather in the family room for a few minutes and share "Praise Reports" and "Prayer Requests" from the day, and then we pray as a family. Sometimes, we discuss a scripture or teach a life lesson.

We have found this to be one of the most rewarding and informational things we have done as parents. Time and again, we have been amazed at what we have learned about our kids -- their thoughts, challenges and concerns -- through this simple exercise.

One evening in the first few months after the adoption, we asked each of the children to share with us one of their dreams for the future. We expected to hear things like what they wanted to be when they grew up, etc.

One daughter shared that she had a dream of visiting Italy one day. This is the kind of response we were expecting. But when we got to Agnes, she said matter-of-factly,

"My dream has died."

There was little emotion in her voice. She just stated it as if it was perfectly OK for a fourteen year old to have only one dream that was now "dead."

Of course, we were shocked and asked her to explain. She went on to share that since learning she would be adopted, her dream was to come to America, get educated, and have enough money to improve the quality of life for her sweet grandmother who had raised her.

Her grandmother is actually her great-grandmother and lived to be extremely elderly by Uganda's life expectancy. When Agnes had nowhere to go during holidays from the orphanage, it was this maternal great-grandmother who had cared for her and taken her in.

Later when Agnes aged out of the orphanage, she returned to her grandmother, who at this point was in very poor health and unable to rise from her mat. This precious woman lived in this condition for almost one year while she waited for our adoption to be completed. She and Agnes shared a deep and loving bond. I had the honor of meeting her and receiving her blessing during our time in Uganda.

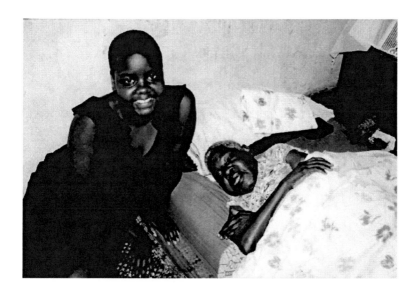

Shortly after we left for the U.S. with the children, she passed away. It was clear she had been holding on, just waiting to see that the children were safely in our family.

Agnes' dream for her life was to be able to financially support her grandmother and give her the care that she needed. She hoped in her heart that her grandmother would remain alive until she could earn enough money to return and bless her. With her grandmother's death, Agnes felt that her dream had died. She had no other dreams for her life and had not even considered any dreams about herself or of what she might want of the future.

Since learning of this deep loss, we have worked with Agnes, slowly, to develop new dreams for the future. Agnes is extremely bright and has a gift for sciences and math. She made the honor roll the first semester she was in America. She also has a deeply compassionate heart and a great gift for mercy. Agnes feels called to medicine and now hopes to be a doctor one day. She would like to be a pediatrician or a gerontologist, because to quote her,

"I love babies and old people."

We have had many talks with Agnes to let her know that her future is bright, and she can be *anything* she sets her mind to now that she has the opportunity of education and the support of a loving family.

Agnes also now dreams of owning her own hospital one day...in Uganda. With our love and guidance, she has allowed herself to dream dreams for her future beyond what she ever thought could be possible. She still has a strong desire to rescue her people, and I believe this dream will be fulfilled with God's help.

Your older adopted child will bear the weight of his fortune. The world is small, and news of his country or his family may reach him. One adopted child I know became extremely agitated one day after hearing news reports of rioting in her country. Helping your child work through the feelings of responsibility created by being the one who was "rescued" will be an ongoing part of your relationship.

As Ruth said to us so poignantly one day,

"I always ask God, out of all the children at the orphanage, why me?"

Our answer is that God must have a special plan for her life, and we will be here to support her and help her find the fruition of that plan.

Lesson 10

God Did It

(believing)

I have prayed a lot about how to write this chapter, and frankly I put it off because there is still so much to say. But God is telling me that others might need these simple stories so I feel compelled to be finished.

So I will leave you with the most important lesson.

It ain't you.

You didn't choose your children -- God did it. God knew who your kids were going to be just as He knew who your biological children would be (if you have them). I believe this with all my being. It's the only way to explain how much you can love an adopted child. You love them almost instantly, the way you love a newborn with all your heart the moment she is placed in your arms. You love them before you even meet them. If you receive a "referral" photo from half way around the world from an adoption agency, you find yourself suddenly and completely in love with the child in that photo. Ask any adoptive parent. And in case you think it can't happen in the other direction, it can.

The day I met Agnes she walked up to me on a dusty hillside, looked me straight in the eye and said,

"I have one question."

"Yes?" I replied with great trepidation.

"If we go with you, will it be forever?" She asked pointedly.

I thought to myself "Oh my! I know the answer to that question, but I don't know what in her mind the *right* answer is!"

"Well" I answered nervously, "Yes. Yes it will be forever."

She took a moment, considered it, and then a huge smile spread across her face.

"OK then" she said, "We will go."

And that was that. Then she took my hand and led me around the orphanage, introducing me to all her friends as her "Mum." And we have been peas and carrots ever since!

There are several awesome books about the theology of adoption. I will leave expounding on that topic to eloquent theologians and experts. But I will pause here to tell you this: believing that God, not your will, is the source of your child's adoption is foundational to building a successful adoptive family. This is true for you and also for your children.

Things will not always be easy, especially at first. There will be crossroads when the reality of it all sinks in and your child realizes that you are imperfect, your family is imperfect, and adoption into your family is not all he dreamed of. Your child may even look at you in anger in that moment and say something like,

"You are not my real family, and I want to go home."

And when that moment happens, without the belief that God is the author of your family, you got nothin'.

There is just no good, effective or even rational answer to that statement except this:

"Well, this is what God chose for all of us, so you might as well accept it. You are mine, and I am yours, and it is forever."

See, adoption can't be seen as a legal contract. Contracts can be broken – even a child knows that. Unless you believe and teach your child to believe that on the day of his adoption a miracle took place, and he was cleaved permanently into your family by God, then a back door is always open. And that back door will lurk in the shadows and create deep insecurities in your child and your family life.

On more than one occasion in the first few months after our children came home, I looked at one in a heated moment and said,

"Sorry pal. This is forever. You are stuck with me as your mother."

And when you keep reminding your child that this is *permanent* because it was done by God (and therefore cannot be undone by man), something wonderful happens. Your child's heart begins to *know* it. Your child's heart knows that you are not going anywhere and that you would do anything for him, just as you would for a biological child.

And your adopted child is not the only one impacted by this understanding. Your other children will experience it as well. I would not know this if I had not seen it in so many adoptive families, but siblings of adopted children also experience the joy of having their hearts cleaved to their adopted siblings in a miraculous way.

Before we adopted Agnes, Ruth and Nathan, Olivia was the baby of our family. After the adoption, people would often ask me in hushed tones,

"How is Olivia coping?"

"Is she adjusting alright?"

"Does she *mind* having new siblings?"

Here is my answer to those questions.

Each of us, including our other children, has been immeasurably blessed through our family's adoption. None of us can even imagine our family now without our new kids. I try not to get nasty when waiters in restaurants ask us now if we need "separate checks" when we dine out as a family. But even with all the trials and complications and challenges, we know our family is comprised just as God always planned for it to be.

This belief also puts an important perspective on the questions that arise in any adoptive family about birthparents and biological relatives. With God at the center of our adoptions, there is no threat or competition in my heart about who is my child's "real" mother.

My child had a first mother. And just as God intended all along, I was called to be her second mother. Her first mother and I are both very real. Each of us had a role in God's plan for her life. Believing that God picked me to be her second mother makes me feel honored and favored and blessed beyond measure!

I don't need to try and "live up" to anyone else. I am secure in the knowledge that if God picked me, I must be the perfect choice for my child. I must have what it takes to be her parent. And during those teenage moments, that is what I tell her!

Your child will ask about his homeland or his relatives. He will miss his town or country of origin. He may ask you if he can return to visit and when. All these questions can seem very threatening and raise great insecurities unless you and your child are both secure in the knowledge that God has cleaved you together and nothing can separate you.

Nothing can separate you from your child if you believe that God put you together. He is yours and you are his. Forever. Write your child's name on your heart and seal it with God's covenant and promise.

And pray with your child. Pray for his hurts from the past to be healed. Pray for him to receive your love. Pray for his relatives, pray for his friends left behind. Pray as his heart leads for those for whom he has a burden. God will comfort him and you will receive an awesome gift -- your child's thankful love.

With God at the center of adoption, everything is still not perfect. But life is never perfect. Each of us is flawed and all families are flawed. We get through life only by God's grace and mercy. But at the end of the day, you can rest knowing that you are living out God's *perfect plan* for your life.

What could be sweeter than that?

About My Adoption

by Agnes Tucker

Early in 2009, when I was 13 years old, God gave me a dream. The dream was about three white ladies that wanted to adopt me. Three weeks after that dream, I was at my boarding school, which was located in Kawempe, Uganda, and I was taken to get passport photos. I did not know why this was happening. Auntie Jalia is the director of the orphanage where I lived. I asked her "Why are you taking me for these passport photos?" She did not want me to know why. After this, we had a two-month break from school. But one thing amazing happened during the break. Just wait to know it.

I always spend my breaks at the orphanage with my brother and sister. One day, Auntie Jalia told me to dress up, that I have visitors coming. I did not know who they were. I went and did what I was told. After that I was prepared, and my visitors arrived in a small car.

There were two white ladies from America, but one was a daughter of the other. They brought some food for the orphanage. Auntie was so happy because of that. I was happy too. We went inside the house and sat down on the porch. They asked me my name and my age plus my class. I answered whatever questions they were asking. Also, they asked my brother and sister the same questions too. Not only were they asking, but they were writing them down. After introducing themselves, the lady was called Jodi Tucker and her daughter was called Mackenzie Jackson Tucker.

They said they wanted to adopt us. But we did not know the meaning of adoption. Auntie Jalia explained to us. Then after that, our answer was yes.

I was really excited because we did not have good care and good food to eat. And I was happy about what was going on, because I thought I would never leave Uganda. But there were many things to work on.

In three days, they had to go back to the States to work on some documents. When they left, we felt so sad and we cried. We never wanted them to leave. They went back but they left us an album of photos. The album was containing pictures of their family and friends and neighbors. And they left my sister with a bandana.

Things kept on going on well and many things went on as you know about adoption. We went back to school, and I told my friends that my dreams were coming true. My friends said "What was your dream?" I told them my dream was I wanted to live in America for the rest of my life. And I thanked God for that.

I finished my 9th grade and I went into 10th grade. Much time passed and things were quiet and I had no hope that we were still going. But God still heard my prayers. I heard that we got our passports and that they would come to get us in September. We waited in September but they did not come at all the rest of the year. But we did not give up.

I took another break from school over the holidays, and when we returned, I changed my name to Tucker on all my papers when I returned. My friends were asking me "What is going on with you? Did you make up that name from a movie or something?" And I prayed for many months.

On my birthday, my new Mum sent me some pictures. The pictures were of my sister's graduation, another sister's wedding and Daddy and Mum. I felt so happy and I couldn't stop looking at them. I put them on the wall of my room. Every day before I went to sleep I prayed over them.

During this time, I hurt my foot. The school took me to a hospital to get a surgery for my foot. A lady who was a friend of my mother Jodi was in Uganda and my mother sent her to see me. The lady called my mother and told her the problem. While I was out of hospital, she sent the friend, who was also waiting for her court date for adoption for many months, to see what was going on with my leg. She sent regards from Miss Jodi.

When she saw my foot she saw I had no good care, and she said she would take me to her home and take care of my foot. She took nice care of me and after she took me back to school. I liked her and asked her if I could have my holidays with her. She promised me she would come and pick me up when school ended.

God Answered My Prayer

As it is God answered my prayers. He really did because Miss Jodi and Jerry arrived finally in Uganda in 2010. I was taken to the airport to welcome them. But before I could see them I waited and waited because power was going off in the airport. We also had to wait because some of their luggage was missing. But finally, I saw them. I was so happy. We hugged each other and cried tears of joy. I liked my Mom and Dad a lot because this was my first time to get my new parents. So they took some pictures of us and went to a hotel and we had a nice sleep.

We had a schedule together. We had to go and get Ruth and Nathan from Grandma's house. And so we did. We were very happy to see each other together as a family. We had to meet the judge on the next day, but they told us to wait and come the next day. So we decided to have a break at the orphanage. I enjoyed seeing my friends for the last time and saying goodbye. It was really sad. We went and spent our weekend off to Jinja, which was a good place, and we saw some falls.

After a few days, we went to get our ruling. But we were not allowed to go in to the court. Our lawyer had to get the ruling for us. She was so nice and friendly. We got our ruling and the answer from the judge was YES! I thanked God and I felt like my dreams were coming true. Then we had to work on getting our visas. We got our visas and tickets the same day and we left Uganda the same day. That was amazing and my sister Ruth cried because she left her friends behind. But before we left I told Ruth not to worry. I told her I thought she would like it.

Our First Day in the States

We suddenly got to the States, and we were welcomed with gifts, balloons and also our new Grandma and Grandpa came all the way from Cape Cod to North Carolina just to see us. That was amazing. They told us to wait to go to bed because they wanted us to see our rooms as a surprise. We were surprised and we saw new clothes organized in the closet, and new shoes and our pictures on the wall. And that really showed that our new parents loved us a lot. But that night we did not get to sleep because we were trying on our new clothes and shoes all night! We finally went to bed but it was so late.

That same night, Grandma and Grandpa decided to take us to a dinner in a restaurant. So we went to have dinner. Since we were not used to the time in America, my brother fell asleep before he ate his dinner. The next morning, our grandparents had to go back to where they lived. They left as they had to drive for hours. But they promised to come back and give a visit soon.

Our parents made us learn important things like cell phone numbers, our address, and where they go to work. They made us do that and we did not want to learn that because we thought it was so much to learn.

Our parents were really having many things to do to get us in school and medical check-ups. The next morning we went and got our school uniforms and other things we needed to go to school. Our mother had to call many schools so that we could get started.

My brother was demanding to get started in school because he had never seen American schools before and he wanted to see them. So my dear Mum worked so hard and got a school for my brother which was so nice of her. My brother started school in two weeks.

The first week he got a note from a girl which was saying,

"Dear Nathan, I like you and how old are you?"

Nathan gave it to me to read it for him and he also showed it to my Mum. We were all laughing because that was so funny. In a few days my sister and I got started in school.

The first week of school we did not like it but then after a while we did like it because the kids were so friendly to everyone. On the first day of school we did not talk to anyone because we were still afraid because it was a new environment for us. We had to get adjusted.

The following day, Mum took us shopping. But because all the things were new to us, we wandered away in the store. My Mum got mad at us because we wandered away. When we got home, we were in trouble the second week in America! Our dad told us to respect Mum and we did what they told us.

The next day, we went to our church for the first time to introduce ourselves. We go to Kings Park International Church which is located in Durham, North Carolina. Before church service began, we went to the front of the church to practice how to be in front of people because my Mum knew we would be introduced. So we got ready to be called and Pastor Ron introduced us as a new adopted family from Uganda. People shouted and cheered because adoption is a very special thing because all God's people were adopted.

That day Daddy took us for ice cream and we were so happy. We went back home and had some lunch. Afterwards we took naps and then the next day we had to go back to school.

It was so good and I got my first Honor Roll Certificate. My Mum and Dad said that was so good and they were very proud of me.

My First Holidays

We had our first Christmas and received our first gifts, because in Uganda they don't give gifts on Christmas, only if you are so lucky. We got many gifts from our new grandparents, aunts and friends. And we ate so many candies. It was my best holiday ever.

After Christmas we had New Year's Day, which is also my sister's birthday. She turned 13. We had fun but for me I had to spend a long time sitting because I was getting braids done in my hair. After that everything was back to normal – going back to school and enjoying the new environment.

And then on January 31st it was my mother's birthday and my grandmother's birthday because they were born on the same day and they have the same names. And I love them so much. After a few months, we had my father's birthday and also we had fun.

My First Adventures

The Circus

We went to the circus one night. We didn't know what it was. None of us knew where we were going apart from my older sister Olivia and our parents. It was a surprise or treat either way because a treat comes once in a while. It was good and I enjoyed it. One thing I never saw in Uganda or never heard about was "cotton candy." I had never seen it before or never tasted it before. Maybe it was there in Uganda but I never saw it.

We saw many exciting and fun things at the circus, like "the elastic girls" who tried to squeeze into a box. And also we saw women riding on elephants. It was so incredible. I enjoyed it so much. Especially because in Uganda, elephants won't let anybody ride on them because humans used to hunt them for ivory. During Amin Dada's (Idi Amin's) presidency, elephants were suffering. Some were separated away from their families, yet families need each other.

Another thing was the horses. I don't know whether we have horses in Uganda and I had never seen them before. I

117

liked the way they were controlled by the lady. There are so many things I would like to talk about but if I start talking about them all I won't stop. The circus was one of my favorite treats in America.

The Beach

Later in the Spring, we went to the beach. It was so beautiful and so nice. We went fishing. We swam although it was cold. We enjoyed running around in the sun, building castles and so many other things that we did at the beach.

We were given a house to use for three days. It was so beautiful and it had a nice view. It was so clean and everything was comfy. We enjoyed playing games like puzzles, cards, dancing and listening to High School Musical. We also watched my favorite movie, The Chronicles of Narnia. It is one of my favorite movies in the whole world, although I haven't watched all the parts of it. But I would like to watch them and I can't wait.

After the beach we went back to school and I made my second honor roll and got prepared for summer.

In the Summer

In the summer, we went bowling. And for some of us, it was our first time bowling. I wasn't good at that game but I wasn't bad and I got a strike. It was mostly fun because we went with the Youth Group from our church, Kings Park International Church. Every Saturday we have Youth Group from 6:00 to 8:00 pm. What we usually do in Youth Group is worship God, pray and listen and pay attention to people preaching. It is fun in Youth Group because it is only for students. And you can bring any friend you want who needs

God. Our fellow students at Youth Group are so friendly, loving and caring. What I want you to know is that there is no bullying because everyone has come for a purpose and that purpose is to worship God.

We also celebrated my brother's first birthday party in his whole life. I am going to let you know why it is the first birthday in his whole life. That is because in Uganda, some people are so poor that they cannot celebrate birthdays. And yet it is one of the important celebrations for everybody. So that was the first birthday celebrated in my brother's life. He was so excited. He got presents like toys. And he had a big day because he went to Chuck-E-Cheese with Daddy and the rest of the little boys he invited. That was such a fun day too. And an adventure to celebrate my brother's first birthday.

By that time we had started swimming for the first time. I learned swimming like in a week. And my brother learned in the second week. My sister Ruthie learned a little because she has a problem with her leg from when she was little. She wasn't born with that problem. She was in an accident and her spine was turned and her hips weren't straight. And she couldn't move at first or even feel her leg at all. She got a little better but we weren't able to take her to the doctor because it was too expensive according to what we had. So in that way her leg is not completely healed. That is why she did not learn that fast to swim.

We had our first swim meet and it was awesome. Somehow it was not awesome for my sister because she couldn't swim. But our parents and her doctor are working on her leg. I know in my heart she will get there and in her little heart what I know myself and what my parents know is that she never gives up. She is so strong but she doesn't know it. She has the potential and the capacity to do whatever she wants to do, although she keeps saying she can't do it. She will get there with swimming in just no time. But only with God's power, love and mercy.

My Second Favorite Adventure – The Mountains

So, the mountains are exciting and fun but also ridiculous. We decided to go to the mountains on a Friday. We had to pack up on Thursday. It took us three hours to get there. The journey was nice and before we got there we started seeing views of the mountains and other nice stuff.

When we got there, the first thing we did was to walk around the house and book our rooms. My sister Ruth and I, we picked a room that had two twin beds and much toys like Barbie dolls and nice pink blankets and bed sheets. I picked that room since pink is my best color. I thought that would be nice. We slept tight and softly like babies, waiting for the next big day.

Since we were going tubing the following day, we woke up early and had breakfast, put on our swimming suits and got ready for the big adventure. We got there a few minutes early since my parents like to be just on time. I was a little bit scared and nervous because I had not done it before and I had not even heard of that word "tubing."

We left our car and went in a van that was similar to the taxis in Uganda. I sat in the back with my Mum. It didn't take us too long to get there. When we got there, everybody picked up their tubes and got ready for the exciting moment. We put our tubes in the river.

We sailed well at first and then since everybody was sitting in their own tubes, everybody had to sail on their own. My younger sister was tied onto my dad's tube and my little brother was tied to my Mum's tube. So, I was on my own. Not only me, but also my sisters Mackenzie and Olivia were on their own.

Like I have told you, I had never done this before and never heard of that word. I sailed through the tree that was on my way, and my tube got stuck. I had to get up and get it out. So I got up but there were so many big rocks in the river that go up and down, and you couldn't see them because the water was dirty. Not only were they going up and down but they were also sharp. I struggled to get on the tube but I couldn't. And by mistake, the tube sailed away. I shouted,

"I need help."

But my Mum and Dad were too far away from me. So I had to swim but I couldn't because of the rocks. The people who were also tubing near me were laughing at me. So nobody could help me.

I started crying and struggling in the water until I heard Daddy's voice.

"Hold on Aggie, I got this."

So Dad sailed as fast as he could to catch up with my tube. Dad got it and put me up on it. And I started sailing while crying. But then in just a few minutes I couldn't catch up again. Everybody was too far away from me and I was going in branches of big trees again.

Just then I heard my Mum's voice.

"Get up and swim or walk, and I will tie you to Olivia's tube."

I didn't get up or respond. Then my Mum's voice got mad. Then she said,

"Help yourself and stop sitting there doing nothing."

Then my feelings got hurt and I started crying again. And I told my Mum:

"I am trying my best."

Then my sister Olivia was so kind that she jumped over and tried to swim towards me. Finally, I was helped and got tied on Olivia's tube by Dad. We had no trouble any more.

It took us hours to sail up to where we were from. We passed under a bridge and sailed. In just a few minutes, we were there. We got some ice cream treats and took some pictures. And then I said,

"That was also a fun day."

And then is when I told my Mum this proverb:

A bad beginning has a good end.

This is to You,

My Fellow Adopted Brothers and Sisters

Adoption is when you accept as your legal guardians or when you join a new family and you are part of the family. Some of us were adopted when we were little or babies, and also some of us were adopted in our teen years.

Those who were adopted when they were babies sometimes don't have problems. But if you were older you might have problems because it takes a while to know and understand each other. But if you do have some problems, I am sure you can talk to your parents about those problems.

For me at first, I had problems with my Mum and Dad. I used to get in trouble at least three days in a week. I talked to my Mom about my background and how I was treated before I came here and what I expected from her. My Mom understood my problems. She tried to get my wounds in my heart healed. She told me to tell her all about my hurt so that I can't keep that burden in my heart.

Some of my problems were private. I couldn't tell them to either my Mom or Dad. My Mom decided that I should to see a counselor. So now I go see a counselor every two weeks or three weeks.

Some times the counselor talks to me about stuff that I and my family should change around. And then things changed. I no longer get in trouble as I used to.

So, what I want you to know is sometimes things don't happen the way you want them to. Some of us also when we come here we change or act differently. I think you should act well and think about where you are from and where you are going.

Also, try to respect your new parents, friends and other people. If you won't be you, who will?

Don't change yourself. Sometimes you see people dressing up nicely and you try to be them. It won't help. Being yourself gets easier and easier. Sometimes at school you join some groups and make a good friend whom you know will help you.

Don't join bad peer groups. Watch out where you are
going at school, although some things are new to you. Try your
best and you will achieve your goals. Try to surprise your
parents by doing your best. I know some kids are smarter than
you but you can do it if you decide it in your mind. What I
know is that everybody can be smart. You just need to
concentrate, look around. There are many things you can do to
be smart like other people.

Be true to yourself and the future will show itself. You
are what you are and that's that. Don't fear failure. Assume
success. Don't rush at things. Relish them.

Also, consider some of my proverbs as your life goes by:

You have what it takes.

Be a work in progress and keep progressing.

Time is on your side.

Having fun counts.

Work and play both.

Do what is important to do and important to you.

Start with what matters most.

Your brain and your gut make a great team.

Rise to the challenge.

Get to know your inner hero.

Search for your values. It feels good to do.

Be unstoppable.

There are no easy answers but keep asking questions.

Please take care of yourself.

And don't forget to trust God for whatever you are doing.

Afterword

My Mother's Day Gift

(blog post May 8, 2011)

Today was a beautiful day filled with all the joys of a Mother's Day...special meals that trash the kitchen, gifts from the "Dollar Store", homemade cards, and even a ceramic treasure from school. As I relished every moment, I wondered what would be the highlight of my amazing day with my five beautiful children.

It came early.

As we always do on Sundays, we went to church. Our service begins with several worship songs, and I love this form of prayer. One of the songs had a chorus that went "I love you, I love you." This was written to be directed at God, but since it was so fitting, I opened my eyes and made eye contact with each of my kids, one by one down the row, and sang the words "I love you" to them.

Back to my eyes-closed praying, I heard the next verse of the songs was "I need you, I need you." I was deep in prayer, but I felt a small tap on my shoulder. Quiet Ruthie, always sitting the furthest from me, was trying to get my attention. She looked deep into my eyes (eye contact is not common for her) and sang the words "I need you, I need you" while pointing at me and smiling.

Pop - there goes my heart bursting.

This may not sound like a big deal to you, but of all my children, Ruth is the most distant.

Since her adoption seven months ago, she has been the slowest to bond to us. She avoids affection and hugs. She won't tell us what she needs. When she first arrived, things were very bad. She had been so hurt so many times that she told my husband "I don't respect any women," and she would barely speak to me. She did not want my love, my discipline, my guidance. She had lived twelve years without a mother she could depend on, so she wasn't going to risk trusting now.

But slowly, very slowly, she has come to open her heart like a blossoming flower. She will tell me things now, and ask my advice, and even hug me every once in a while.

So when she looked at me with those huge chocolate eyes this morning and happily admitted "I need you," I knew we had arrived. I was her Mom, and she was my daughter, and she was OK with that.

My joy was complete.

P.S. She gave me pot scrubbers as a Mother's Day gift...we still have a few things to work on!

More at www.matthew185.blogspot.com

Acknowledgements

There is a story in the Old Testament where Moses (an adoptee himself) is leading a battle. Moses has to hold his staff up in the air in order to keep the army winning. When he got tired, his friends stood beside him and held up his arms for him. (Exodus 17)

Older child adoption is a battle. You fight for your child, you fight for your family and you fight for your sanity. Without my friends and family holding up my arms when I got tired, I never would have won the war.

If you are considering adopting an older child, I surely hope God has blessed you with friends like Deanna Jones Falchook, Lilly Ferrick, Eileen Mestas, Rebecca Phillips, Sharron Stewart, Wanda Neville, Jade Metz, Shawnda Kovacs, Jena Penner, Julie Gumm, Kristie Ray, Michelle Cardwell, Suzy Gilles,

Melissa Busby and Salem Richards, fellow adoptive Moms who will hold up your arms when you get tired.

Words really can't fully express my gratitude for…

McLane Layton for all the children rescued from bureaucracy and brought home to their families. www.equalityforadoptedchildren.org

Carolyn Twietmeyer for reminding me that they are all His children. www.projecthopeful.org

Jen Gash for helping orphaned children sleep sweetly knowing God loves them. www.sweetsleep.org

Kay Helm and Sara Sebyala for revealing to me the heart of Pharaoh's daughter. www.friendsoftouch.org

Elsa Mugyenzi, Prossy Froese, Harriet Nakitto and Grace Naomi for teaching me the ways of Uganda.

Scott and Sarah Lambie for keeping Agnes safe while she waited.

Jalia Kayando for rescuing thousands of children and raising my three kids to be beautiful people before God gave them to me. www.lovegrows.org

Katye Rone for loving orphans and being everyone's favorite auntie.

Ken Eudy and Agnes Stevens for teaching me the power of words.

Yonat Shimron for telling our story so that others might be inspired to adopt.

Pastor Ron Lewis and all the people at *Kings Park International Church* for teaching me that I am no longer an orphan. www.kpic.org

Ray Barnett and *The African Children's Choir* for opening my heart to the children of Africa. www.africanchildrenschoir.com

Jedd Medefind for giving me an opportunity to serve the orphan around the world.
www.christianalliancefororphans.org

Acknowledgements__

All our neighbors, friends and colleagues for their enormous generosity in welcoming our children.

Mom for being an adoptive mother long before it was fashionable and teaching me that I would love all my kids equally.

Carolyn for being the sister that proved that adoption is thicker than blood.

Bryan and Anne-Marie and Amy and Adam for sharing Dad with me.

My kids: Mackenzie, you never say no and your heart is a treasure. Olivia, you are a precious gem, a one of a kind. Agnes, God has a huge plan for you. Ruth, your life is a miracle and an inspiration to others. Nathan, God has put a mighty spirit in you and I know you will serve Him well.

And last as in "saving the best for"...

Jerry, my gift-from-God husband who walks out the Abraham anointing every day and answers God's call every time.

About the Authors

Jodi

Don't feel bad if you have had a little trouble piecing together my life story from these photos and stories. I am a slow learner and it took me half my life to get on God's track where I was supposed to be.

Jerry and I met in early 2005 when I was 43. We both had been divorced and each of us has two children from our first marriage. Bryan and Amy Tucker are now grown and married to wonderful people. Mackenzie and Olivia Jackson were 13 and 10 when Jerry and I married six months after we met! Olivia was adopted domestically when she was an infant and she has a multiracial heritage. So of our seven children in total (so far), Mackenzie is my only child by birth.

Early in our marriage, Jerry and I began volunteering through our church with a project to support *The African*

Children's Choir. It was through this work that we had our hearts broken for the orphan and fell in love with the beautiful children of Africa.

In 2009, I had the awesome honor of being asked to be the coordinator for Orphan Sunday, an initiative of the Christian Alliance for Orphans. **www.orphansunday.org**. I serve today as International Director of this project, and continue to follow God's call to rescue the orphan around the world.

Later in 2009 on my second trip to Uganda, I met our Agnes, Ruth and Nathan after being introduced to their orphanage director by a fellow adoptive parent. They were 13, 11 and 6 respectively at the time.

Jerry and I went back to Uganda in October of 2010 to complete the legal process after waiting over a year for a court date. The five of us got on a plane bound for home on October 29, 2010.

We reside in Durham, North Carolina and our life is never boring.

Agnes

I am Agnes Tucker. I was born in Uganda. Uganda is located in East Africa and is a landlocked country.

I was born on July 1, 1996 in the town of Kampala. I grew up in an orphanage. But sometimes I could go visit my grandma who was in her 90's and couldn't take care of herself. During some of my holidays I used to take care of her. She passed away right after I was adopted.

I was adopted into the Tucker family in 2010 and I was 14 at the time. And they are really doing such a good job as parents although they pass through some circumstances.

I really want to thank God for everything he has done and for the precious new family.

And also to thank my two parents and my new siblings. Great thanks to all of you.

Contact us at www.fastenyoursweetbelt.com

Some Reading

- *Adopted* by Jim Wood

- *Adopted for Life, The Priority of Adoption for Christian Families and Churches* by Russell D. Moore

- *Adopting the Older Child* by Claudia Jewett

- *Both Ends Burning, My Story of Adopting Three Children from Haiti* by Craig Juntunen

- *Castaway Kid, One Man's Search for Hope and Home* by R. B. Mitchell

- *Handbook on Thriving as an Adoptive Family: Real-Life Solutions to Common Challenges* edited by David Sandford and Renee S. Sandford

- *Living in the Promised Land* by Susan Wood

- *Orphanology* by Tony Merida and Rick Morton

- *Reclaiming Adoption* by Dan Cruver

- *The Connected Child* by Karyn B. Purvis, Ph.D., David R. Cross, Ph.D., and Wendy Lyons Sunshine

- *There is No Me Without You* by Melissa Faye Greene

CPSIA information can be obtained at www.ICGtesting.com
Printed in the USA
BVOW031446301111

277243BV00006B/353/P